W9-BGT-439

PUZZLED
ABOUT THE
HOME INSPECTION
PROCESS?

PUZZLED
ABOUT THE
HOME INSPECTION
PROCESS?

Tips to help you "piece together"
what you should know as a
Home Buyer, Home Seller,
Realtor, Contractor,
or Home Inspector

PAMELA J. MCALEXANDER

authorHOUSE®

AuthorHouse™
1663 Liberty Drive
Bloomington, IN 47403
www.authorhouse.com
Phone: 1-800-839-8640

© 2012 by Pamela J. McAlexander. All rights reserved.

No part of this book may be reproduced, stored in a retrieval system, or transmitted by any means without the written permission of the author.

First published by AuthorHouse   02/22/2012

ISBN: 978-1-4685-4949-2 (sc)
ISBN: 978-1-4685-4951-5 (hc)
ISBN: 978-1-4685-4950-8 (ebk)

Library of Congress Control Number: 2012902074

Printed in the United States of America

Any people depicted in stock imagery provided by Thinkstock are models, and such images are being used for illustrative purposes only.
Certain stock imagery © Thinkstock.

This book is printed on acid-free paper.

Because of the dynamic nature of the Internet, any web addresses or links contained in this book may have changed since publication and may no longer be valid. The views expressed in this work are solely those of the author and do not necessarily reflect the views of the publisher, and the publisher hereby disclaims any responsibility for them.

Puzzle Pieces

To my husband Tim, I've learned so much from you in our 28 years together. Thanks for the confidence that I could pull this all together.

PART 1

INTRODUCTION

My name is Pam McAlexander. Having been in the mortgage business since 1986 and working alongside my husband, who's been a home inspector since 2000, I have had a lot of opportunities to offer advice in this field. We have conducted approximately 5,000 home inspections in this time period. We have also worked directly with mortgage companies who provide renovation loans. The services we provide for those types of loans involve a similar home inspection that went several steps further. We would detail out the work needing to be done to these houses, pricing the work using average contractor pricing, and preparing contractor bid packages for the buyers to use to obtain their contractor. We've overseen approximately 3,500 properties under renovation that we conducted the initial home inspections for as well.

My husband and I have owned our own inspection business since 2000. I believe when you have this type of knowledge and you can pass that information along to help people, you should make it readily available. Together, we've found there is a lot to teach people about this process and found this to be the best way to get the word out. We really wanted to bring the home inspection process right to you, as it should occur, without having to be the one actually conducting it. During the entire home buying process, there are many pieces, that when you put them all together, fit just like the pieces of a puzzle. I've created several pieces to this book so that all parties: the buyer, seller, realtor, contractor, or home inspector, can work together to accomplish the same goal.

This book will start with the home buyer and what to check for when hiring a home inspector. Even if you've owned one or more houses in your lifetime, there are still things that buyers never thought to check when they decide to put a contract in on a house. I think you're so excited about the house that you don't think about something as simple as "Which light or outlet does that switch operate?" Also, you assume that your realtor or the seller already knows everything that might be wrong with the house and that they've already brought all the obvious things to your attention. If you're a first time homebuyer and you came from living at home, or were in a landlord situation, you will gain some very valuable information from this piece. The most important piece being: Mom and Dad aren't fixing it! And, you don't have a landlord anymore!!! You're on your own, welcome to homeownership.

Next we move onto the home seller. This process can be so easy for you, as long as you take the time to cover a few simple steps before you even think about listing your house. This piece is geared towards what to look for, how to correct it, and why it's important to take care of it before the buyer's home inspector finds something. Also, it will tell you what your role in the home inspection process should be.

Then we get to the realtor. Most realtors are advised by their brokers on what role they should play in this whole process. Sometimes you listen, and sometimes you just wing it. Know how to prepare your buyer's for the home inspection. Know what to communicate to your sellers to prepare them for the home inspection. Know what should and should not be done at the home inspection (on your end). Understand that just because a contractor made some repairs does not mean they were done properly (even if you know the contractor personally).

For those contractors or "handymen", hired by the buyer, seller, or realtor to "fix things" prior to settlement, know what's expected of you. Know what you're obligated to provide as a warranty of the work you did. Best of all, know who's paying you and when to expect payment.

And for those individuals already conducting home inspections or those wanting to get into this field, there are some very valuable tips that will lessen your liability, educate you more, and most importantly, possibly even help you to get repeat business.

Lastly, don't you think some handy maintenance tips would be helpful? Knowing what requires an annual maintenance and what needs to be checked more or less frequently could also benefit a homeowner. Hopefully, you're all aware of basic tips like making it a part of the Daylight Savings Time to check and change the batteries in your smoke detectors. But do you know how frequently you should change the filters on your furnace or HVAC (heating, ventilation and cooling) system? Do you know what to do or when to call someone if your toilet keeps running or the garbage disposal locks up?

The primary purpose behind this book was to help people take responsibility when buying a property. The secondary purpose was to help them be a little more educated and to try to prevent them from "learning the hard way". Buying a house is one of the largest expenses you'll probably make in a lifetime, so it's best to be as informed as possible with what to expect. I trust that you'll be able to come away from this book a lot more prepared for "the process", or in the case of having owned homes before, a little more prepared the next time around.

PART 2

WHAT YOU SHOULD KNOW ABOUT YOUR HOME INSPECTOR . . .

How will I know if my home inspector is qualified?

Treat this situation like an interview. Prepare a list of questions to ask, so that you can compare their responses to others you will talk to. If you're working with a realtor or a mortgage company, sometimes they can provide you with a list of names to contact. Although you may be provided with a list, keep one thing in mind, they work for you and are paid by you, so make sure you are comfortable with the inspector you choose.

Some common questions you will want to ask are: Do you get up on the roof during your inspections? What do you charge and what am I getting for that cost? How long will the home inspection take? What kind of certification(s) do you have? Are you licensed? If repairs are needed, do you come back to re-inspect once they're done? Do you charge a re-inspection fee or is it a part of the initial home inspection cost? What don't you check as part of the inspection? Do you conduct any other specialty inspections and what are those fees?

Let's start with the question about the roof. It's important to know if they get up on the roof during the inspection. The majority of home inspectors check the roof from the ground, with binoculars. This is not a very accurate means of checking the roof. From the ground, you cannot see if the ridge vents are loose, if vent boots are worn or torn, if there are exposed nail heads that need to be caulked, or if you have "soft spots". When you're dealing with a flat roof that may be sealed or rubberized, you need to be able to check how worn the material is and whether resealing is necessary. When you have a flat roof that's just been sealed, it needs to be re-coated every 3 years. When you're dealing with a slate roof, extreme caution must be used in evaluating this type of roof as slate shingles can slide out of place when weight is placed on them. The only things that should prevent a home inspector from accessing the roof would be height, pitch, or roofing material used. If the roof cannot be accessed from a ladder, or is too steep to climb up on, or as mentioned with a slate roof, these things would prevent a home inspector from climbing up on the roof. It's also possible that the type of insurance they carry may prevent them from climbing up on the roof.

There are other means to checking a roof that cannot be accessed. First, they can check it from underneath by way of an attic. This will enable them to see if there is any rotten wood or split beams, which is usually the cause of "soft spots". Sometimes on a shingle roof, the number of layers of shingles can be determined by looking underneath. Note: only 2 layers of asphalt shingles are allowed on a roof. By checking through the attic, you can also usually see if there are any signs of leakage. Obviously if it's raining the day of the inspection, this helps too!

Next is the question about what they charge and what you're getting for the cost they're charging. Are you getting your report at the inspection or will it need to be faxed, mailed, or emailed to you at a later date? If so, when should you expect it? Is your report computer generated or hand written? Are you going to see all the repairs on the report and then will the inspector summarize the major ones for you somewhere else? Who gets a copy of the report? Is the inspector going to go over the report findings with you? Will he go back through the house and show you everything on the report, or is that done as they're going along room by room during the inspection? You need to know that prices can vary dramatically from home inspector to home inspector. The home inspector who charges the most money may not be more thorough than the cheaper home inspector, but you need to ask these kinds of questions to understand why there is such a dramatic difference in price. Remember, there is probably not a state mandating what a home inspector can charge for their services.

How long will my home inspection take?

You will definitely want to know how long the inspection is going to take. Some inspector's can take 3-6 hours to conduct a home inspection whereas others can be done in 1 ½-2 hours. You need to know why your inspector needs to take so long, or how he can get done so quickly. Again, do your homework in advance, so that you don't go in unprepared and then need to leave because you weren't expecting to be tied up for that period of time. Depending on the size of the house, is what should really determine the time needed to inspect it. If the home inspector is not taking control of the inspection from the start, this can be what causes the inspection time to take so long. For example, there is no reason why a home inspection for a townhouse or a smaller scale single family house takes longer than 2 hours. If the inspector has a process or format that they follow, it allows them to move along the house and the inspection without delay. This means that when you bring the entire family to the inspection and mom and dad are trying to get the inspector to be in the room they're in, and your brother is trying to pull them in another direction, and your sister in law wants them on another level because that's where she is, this is all going to make your home inspection take much longer than it should. Follow the home inspector to each room, let him guide which room and which level you are on and checking and in what order. Most importantly, if you have something you want them to see, save it for when they're actually in that room. I can't tell you how many times someone has said, as my husband is in the kitchen doing a home inspection, "Did you notice this window in the living room?" His response is always, "No, I haven't been in that room yet, I'm in the kitchen." The more you side track your home inspector, the more likely they are going to be to miss something. The most important piece of advice I can give you with this particular piece is, if you have children, leave them at home or with a baby sitter. Children will only distract you and prevent you from seeing and understanding everything the inspector needs to bring to your attention. This is especially true when you know the timeline you are going to be at the inspection. Children cannot be expected to behave and not get board, or be hungry and have to use the bathroom for the 2 or so hours it can take to get a home inspection done. The other important reason to leave the kids at home is that you don't own the house that's being inspected. If anything gets damaged, you're responsible for that, not the home inspector or the realtor. That's the other reason why it's so important to only have the parties directly involved with the mortgage at the home inspection. I realize that you want to show the family the house. I also realize that you may have parents, siblings or in-laws that will want to make sure you're not getting taken advantage of by your home inspector. But in the case of a home inspection, the more is not the merrier. Remember, the more people you have there, the more liability you open up for yourself. It is not the inspector's job to go back behind everyone you've brought to the inspection and make sure they turned lights back off, or water back off, or didn't touch something they had no business touching. If you want them to inspect your house, then don't bother hiring a home inspector. Schedule your family to walk through with your realtor another time, when you're not on someone else's time clock. Keep in mind, your home inspection is not the only appointment the home inspector has scheduled for that day. You want them to arrive on time and be able to focus their time with you so you have to give someone else who hired them the same courtesy.

The next most important question is whether they are licensed or what kind of certifications they possess. Can anyone be a home inspector? Yes, as long as they went through the proper channels of training and certification within their state, if required. Would you pay someone you don't know to inspect your house if they weren't qualified? Probably not, however, how will you ever know if they're qualified unless you get some background information on them, and then follow through to check up on that background. Some states have actually enacted legislation that requires very specific licensing to perform the services of a home inspector. Some do not require licensing however there are organizations that they may belong to that have given them some background to become home inspectors. Two such organizations are ASHI (American Society of Home Inspectors) and NACHI (National Association of Certified Home Inspectors). There is also another type of certification your home inspector can receive and this would be through FHA (Federal Housing Administration) or HUD (Housing and Urban Development). To be an FHA/HUD Inspector, the criteria for background and training is different from the other certifications. You must have a previous construction background and/or an engineering background. Now FHA/HUD is requiring this certification to also have the state specific licensing as a home inspector, if applicable. All three of these certifications, as well as specific licensing within your state, are able to be verified by contacting the issuing authority. This ensures they are still operating in good standing. Remember, just because they're licensed through the state, does not mean they have an extensive background in home inspections. This just means they attended the classes, passed the test/exam. Check with your state issuing authority to find out if they also had to have specific background qualifications before taking the classes.

WHAT WILL MY HOME INSPECTOR CHECK?

As we all know, no house is perfect, and there will be items sited within the home inspection report. It is important to understand that although some items may be very minor, such as tightening a door knob, it is not the home inspector's job to fix the house. There has been many a time when my husband brought something to someone's attention, like the door knob, and explained exactly how to make the repair. He then was asked if he had a screw driver and would he take care of that now. There will be items listed within the home inspection report that the home inspector feels it necessary to bring to your attention. In some cases, those repairs may have to be addressed to satisfy the loan requirements. When this happens, ask if these are items that the home inspector will come back and check upon completion. Some home inspectors may have a repair re-inspection fee already built into the price that they charge. Others, for a fee, will come back to re-inspect once repairs are completed. First, you should ask your inspector beforehand how they handle this. Secondly, depending on the type of financing, and certain repairs needed, your mortgage company may require the appraiser or one of their inspectors to go out and re-inspect. When this is the case, you will be notified by them or your realtor, and there will be a fee for this service as well. So don't spend more money than you need to. Find out if your lender will require and order a re-inspection before you go doing so on your own.

Just as important as what they check during their inspection, it's also important to know what doesn't get checked. Some inspector's won't check the inside of a chimney, a well, well pump, or a septic system, main electrical lines that run from the street pole to your house, or the main plumbing line from the street to your house on public water, or swimming pools. You need to know this in advance so that if you have to hire a specialty inspector for these items, you can coordinate the inspections to occur simultaneously, if you wanted to. Another important piece to remember is that most home inspectors are not there to identify where all your phone or cable lines are located (or if they work). Remember, these services are provided by others and more often than not are not able to be checked unless the seller currently subscribes to them and they have not been turned off prior to the inspection.

When it comes to specialty inspections, or inspections that are not a part of a normal home inspection cost, you should inquire as to whether your home inspector can perform them. For example, do they also do the termite inspection, well or septic inspections, radon inspections, lead, or mold inspections? Sometimes your contract of sale will specifically state that you want certain inspections to occur along with your home inspection. You should know that there are certain inspections that you should leave to the professionals (people who do that type of work and that's all they do). Remember, the home inspector "that can do it all", may not be trained, licensed, or certified to "do it all". Again, different states require specific licensing for specialized or environmental testing to occur. Also, there will always be an extra fee for these tests to be performed.

As a homebuyer, the time you put into finding a good home inspector, will be well worth whatever you pay. It's also important to understand that your home inspector is not Superman or Wonder Woman. They can't see through walls, floors, or ceilings. They can only observe what is clearly visible at the time of the inspection, looking specifically for signs of previous conditions or problems. Let them do their job, try not to distract them, but ask a lot of questions—you're paying for that service.

PART 3

WHAT YOU SHOULD KNOW AS A HOME BUYER...

WHO SHOULD BE AT MY HOME INSPECTION?

Good question!!! I think if everyone asked this question before they worried about coordinating a million different schedules just to set up the inspection appointment, so much time and aggravation could be avoided. The three most important people to have at the inspection would be the buyer (you), your realtor, and your home inspector. Not the kids, not your parents, not the in-laws, not the neighbors. I know what you're thinking, "I don't want to be taken advantage of, I may not understand what the inspector is telling me, I may need to get repairs done and want that person to be at the inspection with me." Although I can fully understand all these concerns, first things first, if you took the time to check out your home inspector's background, you're probably in good hands. Secondly, if your home inspector knows what they're doing, they can explain things in layman's terms, so that you understand completely what they're explaining. Finally, when it comes to repairs, you and your realtor are going to sit down after the inspection is completed and you're going to determine what repairs, if any, are going to be addressed within a repair addendum that will be provided to the sellers. This is not to say that you can't bring individuals with you to the inspection, but it's very important that they understand what their role is and you understand yours—you're paying your home inspector, so let them do their job!

The home inspection is not the time to invite everyone you know to come and see the house you're getting ready to purchase. Schedule a separate appointment with your realtor to be able to show your friends and family the house. The home inspector really does need to have your undivided attention, and the more people at the house, the more distracted you will become. This is especially true for individuals arriving "late" for the inspection. When you have friends and family coming and going, at different intervals during the inspection, the home inspector should not continue to be pulled away to have to "bring them up to speed". Tell them to either show up on time for the appointment, or don't show up at all. Remember, you take responsibility for everyone you invite to the inspection. It really is best if you don't bring children to the inspection at all. Kids are both a distraction to you and the home inspector. Not to mention the fact that they get easily bored. Lastly, it's not your house . . . yet. So if they break it, you buy it! This goes for people you bring to the home inspection. Neither you nor anyone else, other than the home inspector, should be touching electrical panels, electrical wires, turning fixtures on and off, touching thermostats, etc. Your inspector is there to check these items, so it's not necessary for anyone else to be checking them behind him. If you're not sure that they checked something, ask them. This is very important because the house should be left in the condition it was in when you all arrived.

DO I GET A WARRANTY ON THE HOME INSPECTION?

As far as a warranty on the inspection performed on your house, most home inspectors do not offer nor do they supply you with one. Warranties can be purchased through your realtors and they can point you in the right direction. Sometimes sellers will offer a home warranty on the property you are getting ready to purchase. It is important to note that a warranty is not going to replace an aged system. The purpose behind a warranty is to cover items that were in working order and not at their life expectancy at the time of the inspection, but then stop working. I highly recommend that you consider a warranty on the big ticket items (plumbing, electrical, HVAC, roof), due to the fact that there is too much that is unforeseen at a home inspection. Take the time to read the warranty terms so that you have a clear understanding of the exclusions to ensure if it will be worth your while to purchase one. You can always take advantage of service plans with regards to your heating and air conditioning systems, to alleviate large expenses coming up unexpectedly. Finally, with any type of repairs made such as to a roof, make sure that they were done by a licensed individual, and that you are provided with a warranty for the work done. This way, if anything goes wrong, you call them and not your realtor, home inspector, or mortgage company, to get it fixed.

WHAT IF SOMETHING BREAKS AFTER MY HOME INSPECTION?

What if you never got a home inspection and something breaks what would you do then? People are always under the assumption that there is a guarantee from your home inspector if something breaks, or stops working, after the home inspection was conducted. The key thing to remember here is that you were in the house when the inspection occurred. You, as well as your inspector, looked at and checked things out. Were they working at the time of the inspection? So many things can happen after your home inspection. If the sellers or renters are still living in the property up until the date of closing they could have broke it. Or, in moving out, who's to say something didn't come loose or stop working. A great example of this would be a sink trap or garbage disposal. So many people store things under a sink, whether it's the kitchen sink or a vanity sink. When they go to clear everything out from under there, they could bump the sink trap, unintentionally, and would never know anything happened until after you move in and possibly notice a leak. The bottom line is this: you're a homeowner, not a renter. You don't call your realtor, call the seller, or call the home inspector and ask them what they're going to do to fix this problem for you. You find somebody qualified to come in and fix the problem and then you pay them. You don't get reimbursed from anyone for this expense, its part of being a homeowner. If you don't want the responsibility that comes with being a homeowner, don't buy a house.

On the other hand, if we're talking about serious damage, or something that clearly appears to be a disclosure issue (something that was hidden by the seller from you or your home inspector), then you're dealing with a different issue altogether. This is one reason why it's so important the day of closing or even the day before, to do a final walk through on the house, especially if you've had repairs that the seller was supposed to take care of. You might even want to find out if your home inspector, for a fee, will conduct the walk through with you. What may work at the time of the initial home inspection, or be visible at that time, may look very different days, weeks, or even months later before you close. For example, if there was a drought at the time of the home inspection and there were no visible signs that water was ever in the basement. What if we'd had rain since then and at the re-inspection, you now notice some water that may have gotten in. Your first reaction had you moved in without a re-inspection was that your home inspector missed something. When in actuality, he can't miss what he can't see. You yourself would never have realized there was a problem that maybe even the seller knew something about but didn't tell you, until after it was too late. Try going back after a seller once you close, it can be a very difficult and expensive process.

At a home inspection, we hear many "lines" when we find something that needs to be addressed, or in the case of a re-inspection to check repairs made. This is one of our favorites, "A licensed contractor just recently repaired or installed that." Just because someone who claimed to be qualified made a repair or installed something, doesn't necessarily mean it was done right. So many times when my husband is conducting a home inspection for a buyer, the seller will be completely caught unawares by things he finds and will say, "When I bought this house my home inspector never checked that. My home inspector never told me that. My home inspector missed so many things." All he can ever say to them is, "I wasn't your home inspector." Or our favorite line from a seller is, "That was like that when I bought the house." In that case, his response is "That doesn't make it right." Even in the case of a newly built house, you'd be amazed at what can be found. Consider getting a home inspection done in advance of closing on new construction and consider that your walk-through inspection, just to help you create a punch out list for the builder. Most homeowners are more focused on the cosmetic items at a new construction walk through, not realizing that you could have plumbing or duct work that hasn't been connected. You wouldn't know what you were looking for and would have expected the building inspectors to catch the obvious, well, they don't always do that.

The final advice I would give to you involves permits pulled for any work that has been done, especially that work that was used to advertise the sale of the house (i.e. completely renovated, top to bottom, brand new kitchen, deck, fence, etc.). A lot of these items require that a permit be pulled. I think people take for granted that licensed, experienced individuals did the work vs. the "Handyman Homeowner" who did it all themselves. You can do work yourself, however, if you didn't have the proper permits pulled, who's to say you did it right and you did it to code. This involves one simple phone call to validate whether work had permits pulled and inspections conducted by the proper authorities. Contact your local permit office, give them the property address, or sometimes they will require the tax id number for the specific house. This would be the id number that the real estate taxing authority has for identifying your specific property. Let them know how the house was advertised and you're simply calling to validate that the work had the proper permits pulled. It's better to go into an inspection with your eyes wide open, then to "assume" your home inspector will know that work was done properly and to code.

PART 4

WHAT YOU SHOULD KNOW AS A HOME SELLER . . .

SHOULD I BE PRESENT AT THE HOME INSPECTION?

This particular question can be answered in two ways from two totally different view points. First of all, the inspection is not for your benefit and you're not paying for it. Therefore, if you're there, you're probably going to be in the way more than being of any help. Secondly, the home inspector and buyers don't always feel that they can talk so freely when a seller is present. As the actual homeowner, you may take offense to things being commented on, or become defensive when issues are brought to light. Then there is always the justification that "when I bought the house that was like that". Remember, it doesn't make it right, nor does it mean it doesn't have to be corrected. So in this case, no, you shouldn't be present as it will probably make the inspection take longer than it should as well.

On the other hand, if you're present, and a question arises, you're there to answer it. Or, if you're present, you can ensure that the house is left in the same condition it was in when everyone arrives. There may be things you want to ensure the home inspector doesn't miss such as hidden hose bibs outside, or access panels hidden in closets or where the keys are to that locked up shed out back. Or to make things easier on everyone, make yourself available by phone and go grocery shopping or out for ice cream with the kids while the home inspection is taking place. This way, you can leave notes for where specifics are that you wanted to mention and at the same time, when you come back, they could be close to finished.

WHAT CAN I DO BEFORE I PUT MY HOUSE ON THE MARKET?

Honestly, I think if every homeowner would make this their number one priority prior to listing their house, they may sell their house quicker, and I'm sure the home inspection would be less painful for all those people involved. There are some very simple basic steps to take to get your house ready to sell, and we're not talking about overhauling your furniture or repainting the whole house a more neutral color. If you want decorating tips to make your house more attractive to buyers, ask your realtor. Otherwise, these steps involve things that a home inspector may site you for that if you address them yourself in advance of a home inspection, could cost you much less to fix. Remember that once a home inspection gets done and the buyers ask for whatever they want done, you could be dealing with the requirement that licensed individuals (contractors, plumbers, electricians, etc.) correct the problem. This of course will be much more costly than making minor repairs yourself. I'm not encouraging you to fix something you know absolutely nothing about, or something that really should be evaluated by a professional.

Here are the basics:

1. Cut the grass regularly, and keep it trimmed up nicely at all times, especially if the house is vacant.

2. Trim away any trees/bushes that are touching the house, especially around the roofline or gutter area.

3. Remove or repair torn or damaged screens. Screens are seasonal, they are not required. However, if they're installed and they are damaged or missing, most home inspectors will site them.

4. Clear away any/all debris from the yard (old bikes, metal, trash, etc.)

5. Keep "piles" of boxes, toys, or junk to a minimum on the interior of the house, due to the fact that certain areas must be accessible. Don't create a concern that you're trying to cover up or hide a potential problem.

How will I know what repairs to make following a home inspection?

Most sellers feel they have to be at the home inspection so they know what they're supposed to fix. This is not necessarily true. The home inspector will not generally be going over the home inspection report with you as it's not for you, it's for the buyer. Also, you should not expect to receive a copy of the home inspection report. After the home inspection is complete, it will be up to the buyer and their realtor to sit down and discuss what they want to ask for in the way of repairs or compensation for repairs. They will prepare a Repair Addendum to the contract of sale, which will be submitted to you or your agent to go over and determine what you agree to fix or pay to have fixed. If the contract of sale was an "as-is contract", this means you're not responsible for making or paying for any repairs sited by the buyer or their home inspector. However, you as the seller also need to understand that just because it's an "as-is contract", doesn't mean that if something is found at the home inspection the buyers still have to go through with purchasing your house, because they don't.

If you weren't present at the home inspection you may not know or understand exactly what it is that's being requested to be repaired based on the addendum. Some sellers want to then talk to the home inspector for clarification. Remember, the home inspector is not there to write the repair list, he's just there to bring things to the attention of the buyer and their realtor. You really should direct your questions back to the buyer or their realtor for clarification purposes on exactly what you're supposed to be addressing.

The more diligent you are as a seller, the smoother this entire process will go for you. Take the time to properly prepare your house for sale, take care of repairs properly, and save your documentation for repairs you paid to have done so that you can pass that information along to the new homeowners.

PART 5

WHAT YOU SHOULD KNOW AS A REALTOR . . .

SHOULD I BE PRESENT AT THE HOME INSPECTION?

Whether a realtor is present at the home inspection or not, is at the sole discretion of the realtor. However, if the sellers are not going to be home or you're dealing with a vacant house, a realtor should take the responsibility for letting all parties into the house to conduct the inspection, as well as to check and ensure the property was left in the same condition as when everyone arrives, before they lock up after everyone leaves. Most people aren't clear on what the realtor's role is at a home inspection, outside of letting everyone in and locking up behind everyone. Usually the buyers and sellers do not communicate between one another directly as all communication goes through the realtor(s) involved, that is their role.

How can I prepare my buyers for a home inspection?

First and foremost, prepare your buyers to arrive on time, instruct them on whom to bring or not bring to the inspection, and prepare them for what is going to occur at the inspection and how you are going to address any concerns with the seller. I would highly recommend that you not downplay any deficiencies sited by the home inspector, unless this is your area of expertise. Also, keep in mind when you do suggest to your buyer that they shouldn't worry about a specific repair as you have someone you know who can correct it for them, understand what kind of obligation you are putting yourself under. Take the time to explain to your buyers that an "as-is contract" simply means the seller will not be making or paying to make any repairs sited, however, this does not mean that they shouldn't still have a home inspection conducted. Also, by having a home inspection conducted, this enables them to have the means to get out of an "as-is contract", especially if they find something that could mean considerable cost to them to have to correct. Lastly, make sure your buyers understand that the home inspector is not there to move furniture or boxes in order to access things like electrical outlets. They can only check what they can access or visibly see.

If you're the realtor for the buyer, you will need to be aware of the items sited by the home inspector, especially if you need clarification when it comes time to write the Repair Addendum. When you write the Repair Addendum, you will have a copy of the home inspection report to help your buyers to know what they want written/requested. Be very clear and concise about how you word the repair so that your buyer will be completely satisfied with the result (i.e. using a licensed contractor to make the repair). However, if you weren't present at the inspection, you may not fully understand what the deficiency was, exactly where the location of the deficiency was, or how to properly word the repair on the addendum to have it corrected. Some realtors will even bring the Repair Addendum to the home inspection, and write it up right there so that everything is fresh in everyone's mind and if they need to go back and look at something again for clarification, they can. I highly recommend this course of action.

It is extremely helpful if you have the buyer bring a list of questions for things they may have noticed or questions they may have had when they first saw the house. For example, where are the cable/phone lines, where is the main electrical panel, where is the main water/sewer line, identify the location of the front and rear exterior hose bibs, whether there are any crawl spaces or attic spaces that can be accessed, and whether there are multiple locksets with different keys for all entry doors.

Lastly, encourage them to conduct a final walk through prior to closing, especially when repairs were involved. Check the water again, turn on sinks, flush toilets, check and make sure the same appliances that were there for the inspection are still there and haven't been swapped out, make sure they still work.

HOW CAN I PREPARE MY SELLERS FOR A HOME INSPECTION?

Preparing the sellers for a home inspection really starts from the moment you meet with the sellers in order to list their house for sale. Sometimes I will get sellers who request a home inspection done before they list their house, so that they are prepared for the bulk of repairs that could be found when they have the buyer's home inspector come through. This enables them to make the necessary repairs up front and potentially save them more money than a repair sited by the buyers or their home inspector. Make sure water, electric, and gas is on and running through the property, especially if the house is vacant and was winterized. This will help the inspector and the buyers to be able to have all systems and elements checked the first time.

Next, have them move or remove items that would prevent an inspector from being able to access things like outlets or main systems. I realize the sellers could be close to moving out themselves and may have started to box up items. With this in mind, try to keep the boxes away from exterior walls and have them towards the center of a room as this will create better access for the inspector to check things. If at all possible, encourage them to not be packing up while the inspection is occurring as this creates more chaos, distraction, and things to have to work around. If they have crawl spaces or access panels that are not clearly in site or hidden within closets, make this information known to either you or the home inspector. If there are pull down steps for access to attic areas, make sure they can be accessed and that no furniture is in the way. If different keys access different locksets within the house, have those available as well, to include keys to outbuildings. If the stove is being used as storage, remove items so that it can be checked. Make sure they clear their washer, dryer, and dishwasher of items as well, so that they too can be checked for

PAMELA J. MCALEXANDER

operation. Also, remove items from window sills as the windows should be checked for proper operation (i.e. that they open, can remain open on their own, and that the locks work).

Another piece of information to have handy is any documentation they have for repairs that have been made to the house, (i.e. waterproofing of basements, roof repairs, HVAC (heating, ventilation and cooling) units cleaned/serviced). This information is helpful, especially if there are any lifetime warranties, or service contracts you may have in place currently, and whether they can transfer over to a new homeowner. If you pulled permits for any work you had done on your property and you kept a copy of the permit, this could be helpful to ensure a buyer that the repairs or modifications made to your home were done by licensed people and their work was signed off by the respective building inspectors. If you have the manuals for appliances, fans, lights, this too is great information to pass along to your buyer. I personally believe that the more information you can supply to a buyer, the easier and smoother the whole process goes towards getting to settlement and moving on with your new home.

Lastly, make sure that your seller understands that the buyer may want to conduct a final walk-through of the property prior to closing, especially if any repairs were to be done per the Repair Addendum. Also, if any repairs were not done satisfactorily, they may need to be redone. Finally, any documentation that they were provided by anyone who actually did the work, a copy should be provided to the buyer as well. And remember, if your seller is adamant about being present at the home inspection you should caution them about what they say during the inspection. They could say something completely harmless that could turn the buyer off completely from wanting to buy the house. I try to encourage sellers from being home at the time of the inspection as they really are more of a distraction than a help.

PART 6

WHAT YOU SHOULD KNOW AS A CONTRACTOR . . .

IF I MAKE REPAIRS ON A HOUSE, WHAT SHOULD I PROVIDE?

If you make the repairs, normally you would provide an invoice specifying what you did in the form of service. This invoice should then have a fee provided, especially if the seller isn't paying you outright. If your services are being paid for at the settlement table by the title company, make sure your invoice contains a phone number and address on where to mail the check. Secondly, if you're providing a warranty or guarantee on the repairs you made, it should stipulate that somewhere as well. If you are a licensed contractor, you are required to provide a guarantee for the services you rendered and the buyers should be able to call you back to repair something if your repairs did not correct the problem.

If you're being called in to make repairs, you should be qualified to make those repairs. You shouldn't have to call the home inspector to be told how to correct the problem as you should know how to do your job. If you don't know how to correct the problem you're being hired for, maybe you're not the person for the job. Remember, you may have the home inspector or a bank inspector coming back in behind you to ensure you've completed the repairs to either the buyer's or the banks satisfaction. Also, if you're repairing an item vs. replacing it, specify that on your invoice, so that you're not creating a liability for yourself.

I can't tell you how many times I've heard the horror story about the contractor who came out to repair a roof leak and then after the buyers went to settlement and called them back to repair it again, said that the roof was in such disrepair that they would never be able to warranty or guarantee against leakage in the same spot again as they really should have replaced the whole roof. If you don't think your repair will correct the problem, then don't take the job. On the other hand, I've also had contractors who were in need of work, or taking advantage of the unsuspecting buyer or seller and told them they needed to make much more dramatic and costly repairs, which weren't actually necessary, just to get more money out of people.

WHAT OBLIGATION AM I UNDER AFTER THE REPAIRS ARE MADE?

Your obligation to provide a warranty or to be available to the home buyers after repairs would depend on your state's specific licensing requirements. Most work being done to a house requires a 1 year warranty. The key question here is: Are you willing to provide one? If not, then don't accept that job, let someone else do it. Again, someone more experienced may be coming in behind you to make sure that the repairs you made were actually addressed properly. For example, when you're dealing with termite damaged joists in the basement. Whether you sister or replace those beams have a big impact on how you take care of the problem. When you sister a beam, the damaged beam should be sandwiched between two new beams, same size and entire length of the damaged beam, not just the length of the area that's actually damaged on the beam. More importantly, they shouldn't be nailed to each other they should be bolted, to ensure proper support.

DO I HAVE TO PULL PERMITS FOR WORK BEING DONE?

This is not a question for me to answer, but for the permit office for the area the house is located in to answer. I usually ask, are you a licensed contractor or not? This could be one big reason why this question would come into play. Most non-licensed contractors aren't really supposed to be working on existing houses, and they could get caught by going in and pulling a permit. Or worse, they will have the homeowner pull the permit or go under the guise that "the homeowner should have known they needed to have a permit pulled" to take the liability off of them. Most homeowners are naïve when it comes to contractor licensing. Most states require a Home Improvement License. However, some contractors will take the easy route and apply for a builder's license or contractor's license. This simply means that you can build a house from the ground up as you're required to use people who have their home improvement licenses, but you're not allowed to renovate or work on an existing house. Again, the proper state/local authorities should be contacted if there's any doubt about proper licensing. Some states are prosecuting individuals, with fines and jail time, who are acting as a home improvement contractor when in fact they do not possess the proper licensing and insurance to be doing such work.

PART 7

WHAT YOU SHOULD KNOW AS A HOME INSPECTOR . . .

HOW DO I GET CERTIFIED AND WHAT DOES THAT MEAN?

Most states are implementing licensing requirements for home inspectors. A simple call to your state's Department of Labor and Licensing will tell you if you're required to be licensed and what that involves. Or you can check with the National Home Inspectors Examination to find out which states regulate home inspectors and what their state specific requirements are.

Licensing usually involves taking a class with a specified number of hours, and that it should be provided by an accredited company who provides the classroom setting and the testing/exam to validate completion and passing. These companies usually work in conjunction with your local colleges and most can be found online. These classes require attendance, participation in actual inspections, and passing of tests/exams upon completion. Another aspect of licensing requirements also involve obtaining Liability Insurance, and proof of that insurance. You may also want to consider, even if it's not required by your state, Errors & Omissions Insurance (in case you "miss" something at a home inspection and the homeowner tries to come back on you for it). Your next step will be applying for the actual license with your state. These licenses are only good for a set period of time, at which time, you will again need to pay for renewal and provide documentation again that you're still insured. Some states are now requiring "refresher courses" to renew, so check with your issuing authority to validate what you will be required to do or provide.

There are other organizations that you can belong to as a home inspector. Three such organizations are ASHI (American Society of Home Inspectors), InterNACHI (International Association of Certified Home Inspectors), and NAHI (National Association of Home Inspectors, Inc.). These organizations can provide you with the certifications you're looking for. They can help give you additional training and resources as a home inspector as well as provide you with support and services that you can take advantage of. You can obtain more information about these organizations by going online. You can find website information in the Resources Section in the back of the book.

As far as a business/trade name for your home inspection company, applying for a tax id number, or whether you should be a Sole Proprietor, Incorporated, or an LLC (Limited Liability Company), etc., you should consult an attorney and/or your tax advisor on the best route for your needs.

DO I HAVE TO GET UP ON A ROOF?

Each state has its own licensing requirements involving what you're required to check. Also, the training that you receive for your licensing should tell you if you have to get on the roof and what liability you can incur if you do/don't. Also remember, insurance companies may dictate to you in case you fall off your ladder or even if the buyer or seller is allowed to use your ladder or other tools. Do your homework so you don't get caught unaware. Finally, be prepared to explain to a buyer how you're going to check their roof if you're not getting up on it.

DO I HAVE TO PROVIDE A WARRANTY?

How can you possibly warranty any work that someone else did? How can you warranty somebody's house for them? You can't. There are a number of warranty options for buyers and sellers. If you choose to work out something with a warranty company for a buyer, that's totally up to you. I recommend that you leave the warranty companies to the realtors, since they have the background with working in conjunction with them and the buyers/sellers.

With that said, does this mean that a homeowner isn't going to call you a year after the home inspection when their dishwasher stops working and wanting to know your address so that they can send you the bill? Hopefully the buyer you work with has already read this book. If not, you really need to be upfront with your customers and explain to them your responsibility and their responsibility with regards to the home inspection you performed. It is best to get a Home Inspection Agreement drawn up, that they're going to have to sign for you to conduct their home inspection, that way all parties are informed, in writing, and the expectations are already set. Contact your attorney or see if there are any sample agreements provided when you go through your home inspector certification training.

PART 8

MAINTENANCE TIPS & INFORMATIONAL PIECES

EXTERIOR ITEMS: ROOFING

The key is to keep it in tact and sealed up tight, to keep the elements out. If shingles blow off or come loose, get these repaired or replaced as soon as possible. A good rain can cause leakage when this happens.

Roof flashing is something you will find around chimneys or fireplaces on the roofline. If it's coming up around those areas, get it repaired to keep it flush and sealed to keep water out.

Vent boots are another way in which water can get in through the roofline. The vent boots are those stacks coming up out of the roofline where venting is required in bathrooms or with water heaters. These should not be cracked or worn, in this case, get them replaced and then make sure they're caulked to keep the water out.

When nails are coming up on the roofing shingles, they need to be nailed down and caulked, again, to keep water out.

Know that if you have a tarred roof or a rubberized roofing material down, these require regular maintenance with sealing them every so many years. When the time comes for that tarred roof to be replaced, most people opt for the rubberized roofing membrane as it lasts longer.

GUTTERS/DOWNSPOUTS

Keep these cleaned out! I can't stress this enough. Their purpose is to re-direct water from the roofline to the yard. When they're clogged, they don't work. Keep trees trimmed away from the rooflines as these leaves are what clog gutters. When downspouts are not in place, water drains back against the foundation wall (hence water getting into your basement). Water should drain away from the house. Splash blocks are also important in keeping water running away from the property. Clean out your gutters and downspouts every spring and fall as regular maintenance.

WINDOWS

Look for cracked caulking and broken panes. Air can get into the house through either means. Keep your windows sealed and re-caulk as necessary. Replace any cracked glass to prevent moisture build up.

STORM DOORS

These are an extra barrier of insulation on exterior doors. They help to keep the cold out. They're good to have in place and can help keep the elements out as well.

GARAGE DOORS

If your garage door is made of wood, keep it painted or stained on the exterior as well as the interior. This will help to prevent moisture from penetrating the wood from the interior side, causing warping or paint damage to the exterior.

Keep your rollers lubricated and your tracks aligned. If the door seems heavier than usual to open, it could be a spring adjustment, which should be handled by a properly trained individual.

If you have electric garage door openers, test them occasionally to ensure that the safety mechanism works when it comes in contact with something as it's closing, to prevent accidents.

INTERIOR ITEMS: REFRIGERATORS

Keep dust and debris away from the coils (usually found behind the kick plate on the bottom, but can also be found on the back of the refrigerator).

If the cooling coils in the freezer are covered in ice, this can prevent the refrigerator/freezer from properly cooling things. You can defrost them manually by using a blow dryer, but be prepared for a lot of water so you're not standing in a puddle operating the blow dryer. There's a catch pan under the coils, make sure it's not clogged.

The best piece of advice I can give you, DO NOT over pack a freezer. This can cause the cooling coils to cover in ice.

NOTE: Always unplug the refrigerator if you're going to be working with the coils to prevent injury. When in doubt, always contact a company that can repair refrigerators. They will usually walk you thru some steps to take before they send their repairman out anyway.

DISHWASHERS

Keep the drain pipe and sink trap clear of blockages as this can cause drainage issues with the dishwasher. And please, rinse your dishes off before putting them in the dishwasher, especially if you don't want any of that food left on the dishes to clog the drain pipe.

Garbage Disposals

If it jams or suddenly stops working, check to make sure there is nothing stuck inside the drain. Please do not turn on the disposal while your hand is inside and wait for it to stop spinning before you stick your hand down there to prevent injury. If something is stuck, pull it out. If you can't pull it out, you will need to look under the sink at the unit itself and use the "key" to unlock it. When you have removed the object and are able to turn it with your hand down the drain, remove your hand and then push the reset button under the sink on the unit itself. This should get things back to working.

Remember, your garbage disposal is NOT a trash compactor. Scrape your dishes into the trash can, not into the garbage disposal.

Stoves

Don't spray oven cleaner on the heating coil inside an oven, it eats away at the heating elements. If your stove is equipped with a self cleaning mechanism, do not use oven cleaner. The purpose behind the self cleaning mechanism is to heat up high enough to burn off any residue on the inside of the oven. Remember to remove any pans or shelving units inside of the oven before using the self cleaning mechanism.

FAUCETS

Faucets can leak at the base or from the actual faucet opening when seals, washers or o-rings get worn. When this happens, parts need to be replaced. Be conscious of leaks, they can cause more damage than you sometimes realize. If you have a shower diverter that leaks, it's hard to tell if it's also leaking behind the shower wall, so take care of the problem when you notice it, don't just let it continue.

DRAINS

Whatever you do, keep the hair out of the drains, to prevent clogging! Clean out your drains regularly.

Leaking pipes or traps are also possible. Storing too many items under a sink, vibration from garbage disposals, or even continual hot water running through drains can cause leaks. If you're checking under the sink regularly, you'll catch a leak before it causes damage to anything you're storing under the sink.

Toilets

If a toilet bowl or base is leaking, check for cracks in the bowl or leaks at the base. If the bolts are too tight holding the toilet down, this too can cause them to leak. Check your supply valve for leaks as well.

If a toilet is flushed and it keeps running, there could be several causes, all easy to check. Check the toilet float it may need to be replaced. The chain that connects the arm to the flapper could be kinked. The fill tube could be cracked. If you have to jiggle the handle to get it to stop, there's a problem and it's well worth checking into.

HOT WATER HEATERS

There are so many types of hot water heaters; there are tank-less, one's that are operated with oil, gas, or electric. The biggest thing to remember is that if it's operated by oil or gas, there will be a pilot light (meaning a flame). DO NOT store things around this type and make sure they're properly vented (you don't need a carbon monoxide issue). Also, if the water is not heating up, the first obvious sign to look for on the oil or gas operated would be, is the pilot light still lit. If it's not lit, it's not heating the water. With an electric hot water heater, this is a little more difficult in that there are heating elements inside the tank that heat the water. DO NOT turn a hot water tank on unless you KNOW it is filled with water, otherwise you could damage your unit.

WASHING MACHINE

You should check your water lines going to the washing machine annually. I recommend stainless steel hoses. When you're going on vacation or will be away for a long time, turn off the supply lines. Also, due to pressure on the hoses with regular use, change out your hoses every 5 years. Be conscious of kinking lines by pushing the washing machine too close to the wall.

DRYERS

Clean out the lint catcher every single time you use your dryer, this enables the heat being used to be more efficient. Lint build up will not dry your clothes in a timely manner. Remember, lint can cause fires. Because of this, you will want to keep the areas behind, below and around the dryer clear of lint dust as well. Check your exhaust line to outside and keep it free from debris and lint as well. If you have to, put a screen on the exterior to keep birds from building their nests up inside it, this too can cause your clothes to not dry in a timely manner. On your exhaust line coming out of the dryer to the outside, make sure there are no violent bends or crimps in the line, this too will hold lint/felt and can cause build up. Finally, gas dryers must use a metal exhaust line, not a plastic one, due to the extent of the heat coming off the unit, which can melt the plastic line.

ELECTRICAL & PANELS

Carefully mark your electrical panels so you know what breaker operates what items within your home. If a breaker is "tripped", power will stop to that outlet or switch until you reset the breaker. To reset it, just find the breaker that's either positioned in the middle vs. far left or far right, or the one reflecting a red dot vs. a green dot. Move it to the off position and then flip it back to on position. If you have an outlet that suddenly stops working, and you check your panel and it doesn't appear that a breaker has tripped, make sure that one of your GFCI (ground fault circuit interrupter) outlets (which are usually located near water sources like the kitchen, bathrooms, basement, outside outlets, etc.). If a GFCI outlet trips at the outlet, it can affect other outlets that are tied to it. You will have to go to the GFCI outlet source and push the reset button on it. This should restore power to that outlet if the GFCI outlet was tripped.

When thinking about the placement of furniture, be conscious about how close you put furniture against a wall containing an outlet, especially if that outlet is in use. Whatever you plug into that outlet, there must be enough room so that you're not crimping that electrical plug, as they can break off and then cause a fire as well.

SMOKE DETECTORS

Check your batteries annually to ensure your smoke detectors are operational. A good time to remember to do this is Daylight Savings Time. Look into getting combination smoke/carbon monoxide detectors, especially if you have any type of natural fuel burning equipment in the house (i.e. oil, gas, propane used for fireplaces, stoves, dryers, furnaces, etc.). If you have fuel burning equipment, carbon monoxide poisoning is always a possibility.

Heating & Air Conditioning Systems

Keep your duct work/register vents cleaned and free of debris. Ensure that your duct work is always attached (and not hanging unsecured). If you have areas where air can escape, use duct tape (that's really what it's for).

Keep any items you're storing, like boxes, away from any furnace/heat system (especially one with a pilot light) to eliminate the chances of a fire starting.

Remember to change your filters regularly. There are filters that are within the units themselves and then you will have filters in the vents where it sucks the air in. Cheaper filters can be changed monthly and the better ones can be changed quarterly for the filters within your return vents. Check your filters and replace regularly on your units. A note, if you cannot see through the filter at the store, don't put it in your unit as one that is too thick will restrict air flow and can change the calibration of your unit. You can find the filter size to be using on your unit or on the old filter you're replacing. You can purchase filters through any type of store (Home Depot, Lowes, Walmart, to name a few).

During the summer when you're using your air conditioner, if air is blowing through the registers but it is not cold air, check your outside condenser unit and make sure the fan is spinning. It it's not, cold air can't circulate. If it is spinning but cold air isn't coming through the registers, you could have a Freon problem. Remember, when trying to cool a house "quickly" by dropping the thermostat setting in the 60's, you run the risk of damaging your units. Also, when the temperature outside is below 60 degrees and you turn the air conditioner on in your house, you could cause frost to appear on your coils outside, which can also damage your unit.

When dealing with a heat pump, it's not meant to run on auxiliary or emergency heat on a regular and consistent basis, this will damage your unit.

Keep bushes and trees away from your outside condenser units. Keep them clear of debris. With a heat pump, keep the snow, ice and debris off and away from your outside unit, to prevent damage to your system.

The key to longevity with systems is regular annual maintenance. Get your interior and exterior units cleaned and serviced annually.

RESOURCES

ASHI (American Society of Home Inspectors) www.ashi.org and www.theashischool.com or call the school directly at 1-888-884-0440

InterNACHI (International Association of Certified Home Inspectors) www.nachi.org

NAHI (National Association of Home Inspectors, Inc.) www.nahi.org (This site will also provide you with a list of all the different companies that provide the certification/training programs to be a licensed home inspector. They even have a NAHI Certified Real Estate Inspector (CRI) Program for current and experienced home inspectors.)

National Home Inspector Examination www.homeinspectionexam.org (From here, click on the State Regulations box to find out if your state regulates home inspectors and to get state specific information on who to contact.)

FHA/HUD (Federal Housing Administration/ Housing and Urban Development)
www.hud.gov

NOTES

NOTES

NOTES

NOTES

NOTES

NOTES

CPSIA information can be obtained at www.ICGtesting.com
Printed in the USA
LVOW121256011012

301011LV00001B/3/P